Beyond
The Black Hole

Written by Frank Pedersen
Illustrated by Graeme Tavendale

Contents	Page
Chapter 1. *The Cosmos travels into the unknown*	5
Chapter 2. *The black hole*	8
Chapter 3. *Warning!*	14
Chapter 4. *A discovery is made*	18
Chapter 5. *Mutiny*	28
Verse	32

Beyond
The Black Hole

With these characters ...

Commander Gruder

Officer Yanna

Officer Hardy

Officer Chang

"We are doomed

Setting the scene ...

Step into the future! It is the year 2359, and the crew of the spacecraft *Cosmos* is heading into deep space to search for minerals on uninhabited planets. They are traveling into dangerous, unknown territory. Soon, they will be flung into distant galaxies and solar systems. The people on board the *Cosmos* will be faced with life-threatening decisions. No matter what happens, someone will get into deep trouble. With only the video log to tell the story, *you* will have to judge for yourself who was right and who was wrong!

We cannot escape."

"Log Entry:
June 10, 2359. Time: 8:00 A.M.
This is a record of the last journey of the intergalactic mining spacecraft *Cosmos*. You may not believe what follows, but I shall tell it as it happened. I am the commander of the *Cosmos*, and my name is Yanna. The craft's records show that I started this voyage as the biological officer. The biological officer is a scientist who studies the living things we discover on our voyages.

As the story unfolds, you will see why our original commander is no longer in charge. If we ever reach our home planet again, I hope this record will serve as an explanation for my actions. I am to be charged with mutiny. Mutiny is a very serious charge."

Chapter 1.

The *Cosmos* was an enormous spacecraft. Its purpose was to find uninhabited planets and then return to its home planet with all the minerals it could mine from those distant worlds. The *Cosmos* obtained the minerals by vaporizing entire planets and sucking the useful pieces into its huge cargo hold. After the *Cosmos* had filled its cargo hold, all that was left of a planet was dust.

"Log Entry by Commander Gruder: April 14, 2359. Time: 9:15 A.M. We have been traveling at a high speed for weeks now. With our cargo hold empty, we can cover great distances. We are traveling to remote areas of the galaxy in search of mineral resources. Our power reserves are full. My crew and I are hoping for great success on this exploration."

The *Cosmos* was launched from its home planet to search for badly needed energy resources. After years of constant mining and vaporization, the inner parts of the galaxy were depleted. The search for more resources had to move to very distant, unknown areas of the galaxy.

"Log Entry by Communications Officer Hardy: April 17, 2359. Time: 5:00 P.M.
We are at such a great distance from the home planet that communication is very difficult. The signals we receive from home are very weak. As we move to the unknown edge of the galaxy, we are experiencing a lot of interference from an unknown radio source. It is very mysterious. Strange things are happening with our communication instruments. My technicians are working around the clock to solve the problems."

Chapter 2.

In deep space, the *Cosmos* passed through very old solar systems. In many, the central star was so old that it was starting to collapse. As the central stars collapsed, the gases and other matter that made up the stars were under enormous pressure. They became dangerous. In some solar systems, powerful whirlpools of energy and matter were created. These places have struck fear into space travelers since we were first able to leave our planet. We know them as black holes.

"Log Entry by Navigation Officer Chang: May 21, 2359. Time: 4:05 P.M.

As we move deeper and deeper into unknown areas of space, our star maps and navigational methods become more and more unreliable. We try to keep the *Cosmos* on a straight course. It's difficult because the stars and solar systems orbit and move position much faster than they do in the known areas of the galaxy. Soon, we may be lost. But we must continue our mission and hope that we are able to find our way back to the home planet."

Black holes are impossible to see until it is too late. By the time you recognize a black hole, you are trapped in its gravitational pull. You cannot escape. You are drawn into the center of the space whirlpool. The rules of time no longer work. You are sucked into the black hole at the speed of light. No one has ever been known to return.

"Emergency Entry by Commander Gruder:
May 22, 2359. Time: 7:00 A.M.
Our normal engine power is weakened and we are being drawn into an orbit that is difficult to escape. Although we must be orbiting *something*, we are unsure of its location. I have placed all crew on emergency alert. Communications Officer Hardy is transmitting distress signals. Navigation Officer Chang is unable to find our location. We are experiencing terrible difficulties."

An invisible black hole trapped the *Cosmos* in its gravitational pull. Not even the strongest, most powerful spacecraft could escape such a situation. The *Cosmos* spun around and around at great speeds, like a small insect trapped in a whirlpool of water going down a drain.

Soon, the *Cosmos* was traveling so fast that it was approaching the speed of light. At that speed, someone might catch only a glimpse of where the *Cosmos* had been a few seconds before—not where it actually was. As the spacecraft approached the center of the black hole, time started to go backward, and the *Cosmos* disappeared.

"Emergency Entry by Commander Gruder: May 22, 2359. Time: 8:20 A.M. We are doomed. Our biological officer, Yanna, advises that none of us can survive these extremely fast speeds. We cannot escape. The *Cosmos* is shaking apart. We are doomed. Doomed. doomed are We . . . apart shaking is *Cosmos* The . . . escape cannot We . . . speeds fast . . ."

Chapter 3.

The *Cosmos* tumbled out of the other side of the black hole at such a fast speed that the crew saw stars that looked like lines of light instead of tiny circles. Commander Gruder struggled to keep the spacecraft under control, and gradually it stopped spinning. Slowly, it reduced speed and finally shuddered to a stop. Commander Gruder ordered everyone to report in.

"Damage Report by Communications Officer Hardy: May 22, 2359. Time: 8:25 A.M. Everything appears normal, but we are unable to receive any communication from the home planet."

"Damage Report by Navigation Officer Chang: May 22, 2359. Time: 8:26 A.M. All systems appear to be functioning. Unable to confirm our location. This galaxy does not match any on our computer."

"Damage Report by Biological Officer Yanna: May 22, 2359. Time: 8:27 A.M. All crew members are safe. Apart from minor injuries, everyone is alive and well."

At that moment, the spacecraft's computer flashed an urgent warning. "Collision imminent!" A huge spaceship the size of the *Cosmos* was approaching fast. And it was on a collision course with the *Cosmos*. Unless the crew immediately changed their course to avoid the spaceship, it would smash right into them. The commander powered up the engines and forced the *Cosmos* into a sharp right turn. The mystery spaceship sped closer and closer. The entire *Cosmos* shook and shuddered from the slipstream of the other spaceship as it passed by.

"Communication Report by Communications Officer Hardy: May 22, 2359. Time: 8:28 A.M. Unidentified spaceship alerted to imminent collision. No response. Tried to establish emergency contact. No response. After collision avoided, received unidentified communication from spaceship. Message: 'Warning: Turn back.'"

Chapter 4.

The commander of the *Cosmos* decided to move on. The crew needed to draw a map of the surrounding stars and solar systems in order to determine their position. Although the navigation officer reported that the planets and stars were made of familiar materials, they were still not known. Then, the navigation officer sent a secret coded message to the commander.

"Resource Report by
Navigation Officer Chang:
May 22, 2359. Time: 10:15 A.M.
SECRET!
Scanning of the surrounding planets has revealed organic energy resources. Although we have not seen organic energy for many centuries on the home planet, we are receiving computer readings of them in great abundance in this unknown solar system. The organic energy resources are . . . OIL and NATURAL GAS! I don't need to remind you how rare these organic energy resources are. We have discovered a fortune in resources here."

The commander was stunned. Oil and gas were among the most valuable resources in the universe. No one had found any on the home planet for hundreds of years. And they were extremely rare on other planets, too. The commander could become unbelievably rich—if only he could vaporize the source and find his way home.

"Senior Crew Meeting by Commander Gruder: May 22, 2359. Time: 1:00 P.M.

I have told only the senior crew about our discovery. We are about to become fabulously rich. We have discovered the largest source of natural energy resources known in the galaxy and everyone is excited. The only warning comes from Biological Officer Yanna. She tells us that if there was enough life millions of years ago to create these organic reserves, there is a chance that life might still exist on the planet. We are not allowed to destroy planets with life, but we are in a remote part of the galaxy. We must take a chance and hope that no one will find out."

The *Cosmos* continued its scanning of the unknown solar system until it found out that the third planet from the star was the source of the organic material. It was a small blue and green planet that would easily be vaporized and stored in the spacecraft's cargo hold. The commander prepared to charge up the vaporizers. The *Cosmos* positioned itself for the blast.

"Emergency Report by Biological Officer Yanna: May 22, 2359. Time: 4:00 P.M.
I am extremely concerned by the commander's actions. I am still awaiting the results of my own biological scans of the blue and green planet. We must not destroy a planet where there is life. We must do nothing until my data is collected. The commander is ignoring my warnings."

The *Cosmos* began to hum as all the spacecraft's available energy was directed into the huge vaporizers. It would take an enormous blast of energy to reduce an entire planet to dust. Within minutes, the *Cosmos* would be ready to vaporize the blue and green planet.

"Extreme Emergency Report Warning by Biological Officer Yanna:
May 22, 2359. Time: 6:00 P.M.
The results are confirmed. The blue and green planet has life. What is extremely alarming is that the blue and green planet has exactly the same computer readings as our own home planet. Same minerals. Same organic materials. Same atmosphere. If I had received these readings in our own galaxy, I would believe that we were about to vaporize our *own* planet. I must stop the commander immediately. I have my suspicions that he could be about to do something disastrous."

Yanna collected her weapon from the safety case and raced up to the command center. The commander spun around in his chair and stared at Yanna.

"You must not stop us," he said slowly. "No life can be as important as the resources on that planet. We'll be rich!"

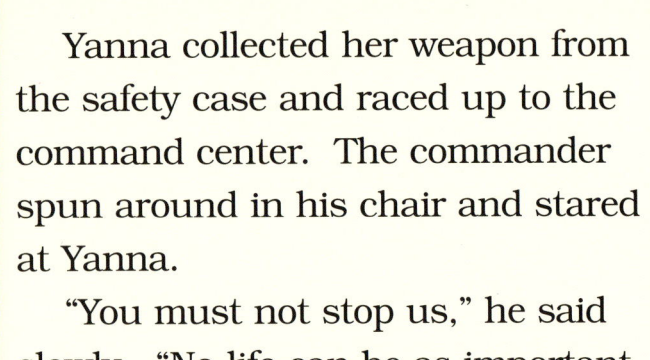

He reached for his weapon, but Yanna drew her own and aimed it at the commander.

"Capture this man," she shouted to the nearby security officer. "He's making the wrong decision. He is about to kill us all."

Chapter 5.

"Log Entry by Commander Yanna:
May 23, 2359. Time: 6:00 A.M.
I have taken control of the spacecraft *Cosmos*. The commander and the senior crew are all under arrest. The commander will no doubt charge me with mutiny. But I have very good reasons for my actions.

I believe that as we passed through the black hole, we traveled back through time. We are not in a strange solar system. We are in our *own* solar system, but thousands of years ago!

Our computer is currently calculating the known movement of all planets in our own home solar system—**back to the past**. My guess is that the computer will eventually find that our own planets were in the same position as those we now see thousands of years ago. If I am wrong, then I will be guilty of mutiny. But if I am right ... we almost destroyed our own planet. And if we were to destroy our own planet, we would have destroyed our own ancestors. We would have never existed!

The results may take many hours, but it is important that we do not remain here any longer. We must try to locate the black hole once more and attempt to travel through it and back into our own time again. I have ordered us to retrace our course at maximum power."

The *Cosmos* slowly turned around in space and with a slow, steady surge, headed back toward the edge of the solar system. It gathered speed and roared past the outer planets. At top speed, the *Cosmos* was shuddering and shaking, but still Commander Yanna powered the engines. Then, suddenly, the spacecraft's computer flashed an urgent warning. "Collision imminent!" A huge spaceship the size of the *Cosmos* was approaching fast. And it was on a collision course with the *Cosmos*!

"Communication Report by Acting Communications Officer Wilkin: May 23, 2359. Time: 6:30 A.M.

Message Sent: 'Warning: Turn back.'"

The huge spaceship turned right and missed the *Cosmos*. Commander Yanna caught a glimpse of its name as it sped past. It *was* the *Cosmos*! Strange things happen when you travel through time. You may not believe what Yanna says, but the log book tells it as it happened.

31

"We are doomed. We cannot escape."

A perfect planet
escapes destruction today.
We live tomorrow.